Ghee's ®

2620 Centenary Blvd. #3-205
Shreveport, LA 71104
(318) 226-1701

A
Companion
Project Book
For
Texture
With
Textiles

By Linda McGehee

**Traditional embellishments
once considered too
difficult to construct
are now easily
accomplished and
fun to create.**

ISBN# 09637160-1-8

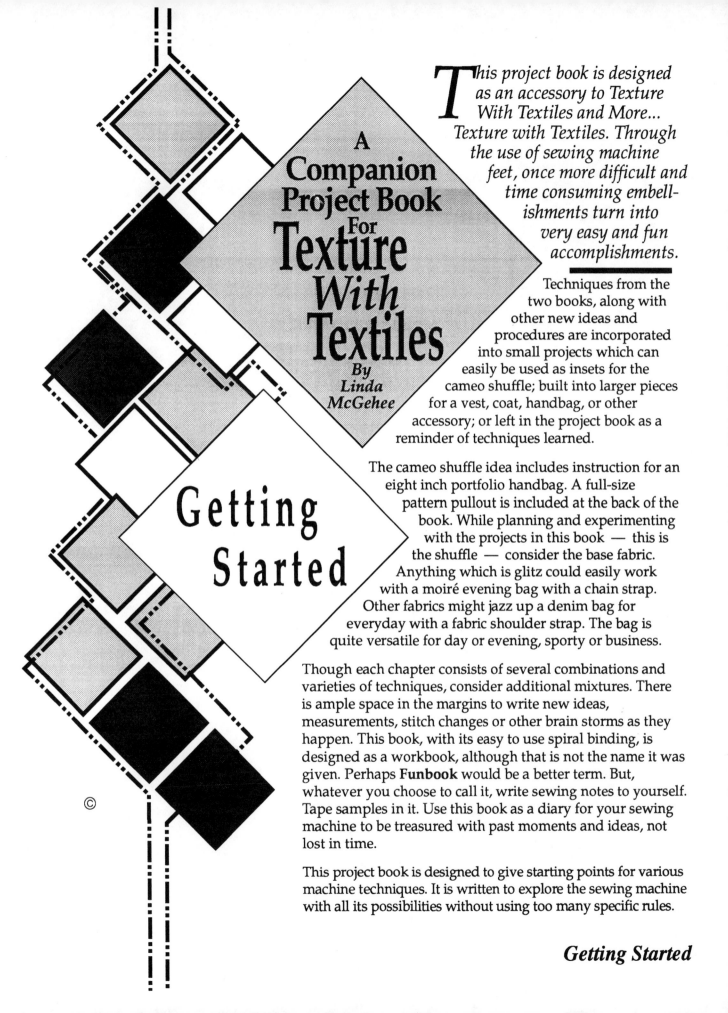

A Companion Project Book For **Texture With Textiles**

By Linda McGehee

Getting Started

*T*his project book is designed as an accessory to Texture With Textiles and More... Texture with Textiles. Through the use of sewing machine feet, once more difficult and time consuming embellishments turn into very easy and fun accomplishments.

Techniques from the two books, along with other new ideas and procedures are incorporated into small projects which can easily be used as insets for the cameo shuffle; built into larger pieces for a vest, coat, handbag, or other accessory; or left in the project book as a reminder of techniques learned.

The cameo shuffle idea includes instruction for an eight inch portfolio handbag. A full-size pattern pullout is included at the back of the book. While planning and experimenting with the projects in this book — this is the shuffle — consider the base fabric. Anything which is glitz could easily work with a moiré evening bag with a chain strap. Other fabrics might jazz up a denim bag for everyday with a fabric shoulder strap. The bag is quite versatile for day or evening, sporty or business.

Though each chapter consists of several combinations and varieties of techniques, consider additional mixtures. There is ample space in the margins to write new ideas, measurements, stitch changes or other brain storms as they happen. This book, with its easy to use spiral binding, is designed as a workbook, although that is not the name it was given. Perhaps **Funbook** would be a better term. But, whatever you choose to call it, write sewing notes to yourself. Tape samples in it. Use this book as a diary for your sewing machine to be treasured with past moments and ideas, not lost in time.

This project book is designed to give starting points for various machine techniques. It is written to explore the sewing machine with all its possibilities without using too many specific rules.

Instead, use the basic information and adapt it for creative choices. There are no wrong techniques, just endless possibilities.

To create new projects, designers are constantly trying new ideas. One thing always leads to another. So try something. *Anything.* At least a decision can be made as to whether the *anything* is suitable for further adventure.

As you begin to learn and experiment with your sewing machine, allow yourself the freedom of breaking a few rules from past projects, playing with the stitch width and length, trying combinations with memory, or simply having fun with the wonderful stitches that are on the machine.

Enjoy the fun and adventure that go along with sewing in the '90's. With the machines, feet, tools, fabrics, trims, laces, threads, yarns, and interfacings that are available today everyone can be creative. Once YOU start, you will be amazed how much easier the next row is. And until you have tried something you have no idea how easy it really can be.

So let's begin...

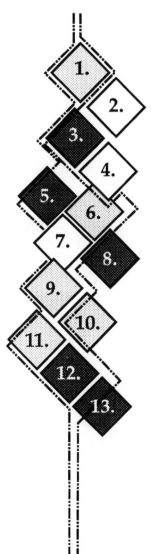

Table of Contents

This book is arranged by subject matter. The chapter title is stated in the right corner of each page for easy referencing. A 5" x 5" square is incorporated into each chapter for placement of your completed sample.

Introduction

Through the Eye of a Needle: *Essential information regarding sewing machine needles*

Lessons

    1. Couching

    2. Couching Too

    3. Fringe It

    4. Pintuck With A Goose

    5. Ticker Tape Appliqué

    6. Mono-Pintuck

    7. Leaf Appliqué

    8. Cutwork

    9. Traditional Appliqué Made Easy

    10. Reverse Appliqué

    11. Rail Fence

    12. Combining

Putting It All Together: *Instructions, Cutting Layout and Pattern*

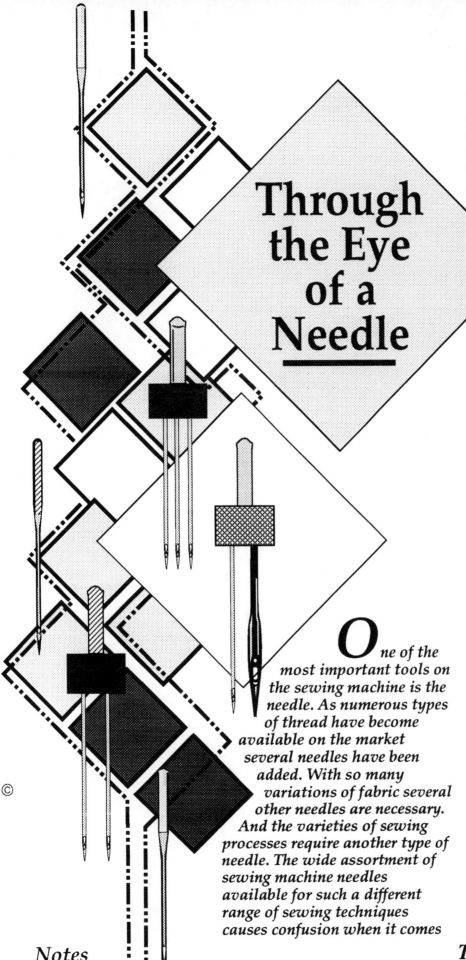

Through the Eye of a Needle

*O*ne of the most important tools on the sewing machine is the needle. As numerous types of thread have become available on the market several needles have been added. With so many variations of fabric several other needles are necessary. And the varieties of sewing processes require another type of needle. The wide assortment of sewing machine needles available for such a different range of sewing techniques causes confusion when it comes

Notes

to selecting the correct size and type for a project.

To make the decision easier for selecting the proper needle type and size, refer to these guide lines. Many new needles have been introduced to accommodate the wide range of fabrics, threads and techniques. Be certain the best needle is used to complete the task in the easiest and most timely manner.

Needles are not designed to last forever. They must be changed frequently, usually every six to eight sewing hours. A needle becomes blunt from use as well as abuse. Sewing on buttons, charms, and beads improperly may shorten the life of a needle. Always sew with a good needle to prevent damage to the fabric and machine.

The numbering system on the needle packaging refers to the size of the needle. Not every type of needle is available in a wide variety of sizes, but the listing will act as a guide to help determine the correct size:

8/60	sheer fabrics, fine lace, silk
9/65	batiste, chiffon, organdy
10/70	crepe de chine, lawn, handkerchief linen
11/75	challis, cotton knits, wool jersey
12/80	muslin, chintz, velvet, synthetic suede
14/90	textured linen, quilted fabrics, flannel
16/100	denim, sailcloth, fake fur, ticking
18/110	upholstery, canvas, drapery fabrics
19/120	work denim, very heavy fabrics

The American numbers, the first number, and European numbers, the

number following the slash, are printed on the cover. The smaller numbers (8/60 and 9/65) are used with lightweight fabrics, while the larger numbers (18/110 and 19/120) are used with heavier fabrics. The most common needle (12/80) is used for general sewing with medium weight fabric.

Point of Interest
The upper portion of some needle packaging is a magnifier to assist in reading the needle size.

Ball Point Needle, with its medium ball point, shifts the fibers rather than piercing them, to avoid tiny holes on knitted fabrics.

Embroidery Needle features a specially designed scarf and eye to eliminate skipped stitches and thread breakage with rayon and lame threads. A red dot on the needle between the scarf and shaft differentiates the Embroidery Needle from other needles.

Jeans/Denim Needle, a large size tapered sharp point, penetrates several layers of heavy denim weight or densely woven fabrics without breaking. It is suitable for sewing tapestry and other home decoration fabrics.

Leather Needle has a wedge-shaped point designed to penetrate leather, vinyl, and other plastic or non-woven material. Expect a permanent hole to remain in the fabric if the thread needs to be ripped out.

Metallica Needle is designed with an elongated eye and special shaft to allow fragile metallic threads to pass, creating a more even fill of

pattern stitches and eliminating skipped stitches or breakage.

Microtex/Sharps Needle, with its tapered sharp point, is designed to penetrate silk and microfiber fabrics. It is best for topstitching and edgestitching perfectly straight stitches. A purple dot between the scarf and shaft distinguishes the Microtex Needle from other needles.

Overlock Needle, designed for serger machines which take regular machine needles, has a sharp point suitable for all fabrics. Choose the needle system recommended by the manufacturer.

Quilting Needle, with its special tapered point, penetrates the layers of piecing and seaming in quilting or patchwork. A green dot between the scarf and shaft of the needle is a distinguishing mark on Quilting Needles.

Self-Threading Machine Needle, a general purpose needle, is helpful for persons having difficulty threading regular machine needles. A small slot or opening at the side of the eye allows

Notes
Through the Eye of
a Needle

the thread to easily pass into the eye. The needle is weaker than normal machine needles.

Spring Embroidery Needle is designed for free motion embroidery stitching and quilting. Without a presser foot, the spring prevents the needle from drawing up the fabric, allowing the freedom to meander throughout the project. The needles are available in Universal for woven; Stretch for knits and elasticized fabrics; and Denim for heavy wovens.

Stretch Needle, with its special construction, passes between fibers in the fabric rather than piercing them, making it suitable for synthetic suedes and elastic knitwear fabrics eliminating skipped stitches.

Topstitching Needle has an extra large, elongated eye and a large groove in the shaft to allow buttonhole twist thread, two strands of all purpose thread or up to three strands of decorative thread to pass through fabric without breaking or fraying.

Universal Point Needle is designed for both woven and knit fabric. The slight ballpoint makes the needle ideal for most garment construction.

Wing Needle, which looks like a serpents head or wings, spreads the fibers in the fabric to create holes as the design is stitched. Much like hemstitching in heirloom sewing, the needle can produce many special effects to resemble very tedious handwork.

Point of Interest

Double and triple needles are designed for zigzag machines which thread front to back.

Double Needle has two universal needles with a cross bar attached to a single shaft to allow two rows of perfectly parallel stitching. The first number on the packaging with a decimal point refers to the distance between the two needles. The space can vary from 1.6, 2.0, 2.5, 3.0, 4.0, to 6.0 mm. The second number refers to the needle size. These numbers, the distance and the needle size are printed on the cross bar for convenience. Designed for pintucks and topstitching, the needle can be used for decorative stitching depending upon the distance between the needles and the opening of the throat plate on the machine. A single bobbin accommodates both needles.

Double Denim Needle, with its two denim needles, a cross bar and a single shaft, is ideal for topstitching and embellishing denims, tapestry, synthetic suede, and other closely woven fabrics.

Double Machine Embroidery Needle has two embroidery needles with a cross bar attached to a single shaft. Use with metallic, rayon, and lamé threads.

Double Wing Needle has one wing needle and one universal needle with a cross bar attached to a single shaft. The needle is designed to add interest to heirloom and other fine French sewing techniques.

Through the Eye of a Needle

Stretch Double Needle has two stretch needles with a cross bar attached to a single shaft. Prevent skipped stitches and tiny holes in knit or stretch fabrics.

Triple Needle stitches three rows at a time instead of one or two. Three needles are attached to a cross bar and a single shaft. The first number on the packaging with a decimal refers to the distance between the first and last needle. The second number refers to the size. Like the double needle, the triple needle is limited in stitch width decoration by the size of opening in the throat plate.

Final Points of Interest

With embellishment sewing, you may find yourself changing the needle frequently for different techniques. If the variety of needles seems puzzling to you, remember a few basic rules: Choose

- *the needle point compatible to the fabric*

- *the needle size according to the weight of the fabric*

- *the needle type for the design purpose*

Lagniappe: An old Creole word for "something extra and unexpected"

- the Embroidery Needle has a red dot by the shaft

- the Microtex/Sharp Needle differentiates with a purple dot

- the Quilting Needle has a green distinguishing dot

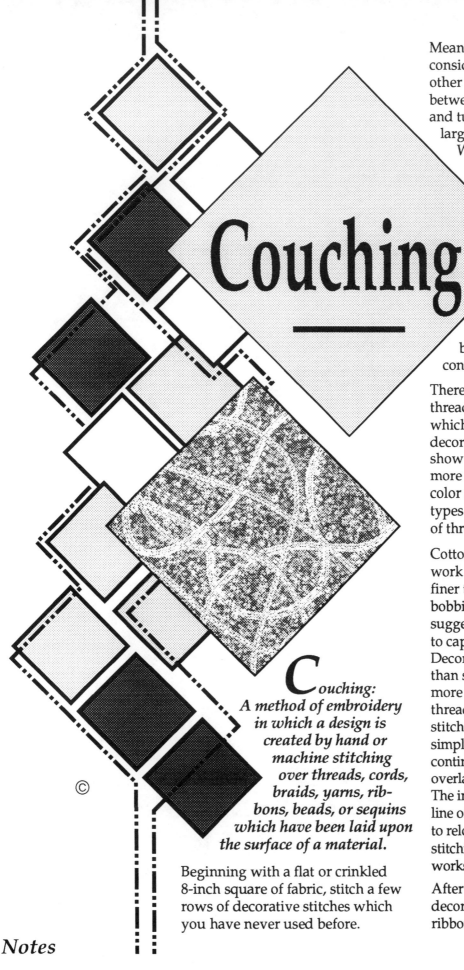

Couching

C ouching:
*A method of embroidery
in which a design is
created by hand or
machine stitching
over threads, cords,
braids, yarns, rib-
bons, beads, or sequins
which have been laid upon
the surface of a material.*

Beginning with a flat or crinkled 8-inch square of fabric, stitch a few rows of decorative stitches which you have never used before.

Meander over the fabric without consideration of straight lines. In other words, sew crooked. Stitch between and around the wrinkles and tucks. Fold back or open up a large tuck to add more dimension. Wander around the design in the printed fabric. Use the mirror image. Or combine several stitches with memory.

Use rayon, metal- lic, or lamé thread in the embroidery needle. This is a larger eye needle to accommodate the fragile threads, preventing breakage that happens in a conventional smaller eye needle.

There are a variety of multi-colored threads, whether metallic or rayon, which work beautifully with decorative stitches. Satin stitches show bolder color change while more open stitches give a subdued color change. It is okay to use both types of stitches as well as a variety of thread types in the same project.

Cotton embroidery or bobbin thread work well in the bobbin. They are finer than most threads allowing the bobbin to hold more. Another suggestion is to fill several bobbins to capacity before beginning. Decorative stitches use more thread than straight stitches. Nothing is more aggravating than to run out of thread in the middle of a row of stitches. But, when this happens, simply rethread the bobbin and continue. As another row is stitched, overlap or intersect the skipped stitch. The intersection will hide the broken line of stitches and it is not necessary to relocate the needle into the stitching pattern. This is a trick which works well when a thread breaks, too!

After sewing several rows of decorative stitches, add $1/8$ inch ribbon using the braiding foot, or

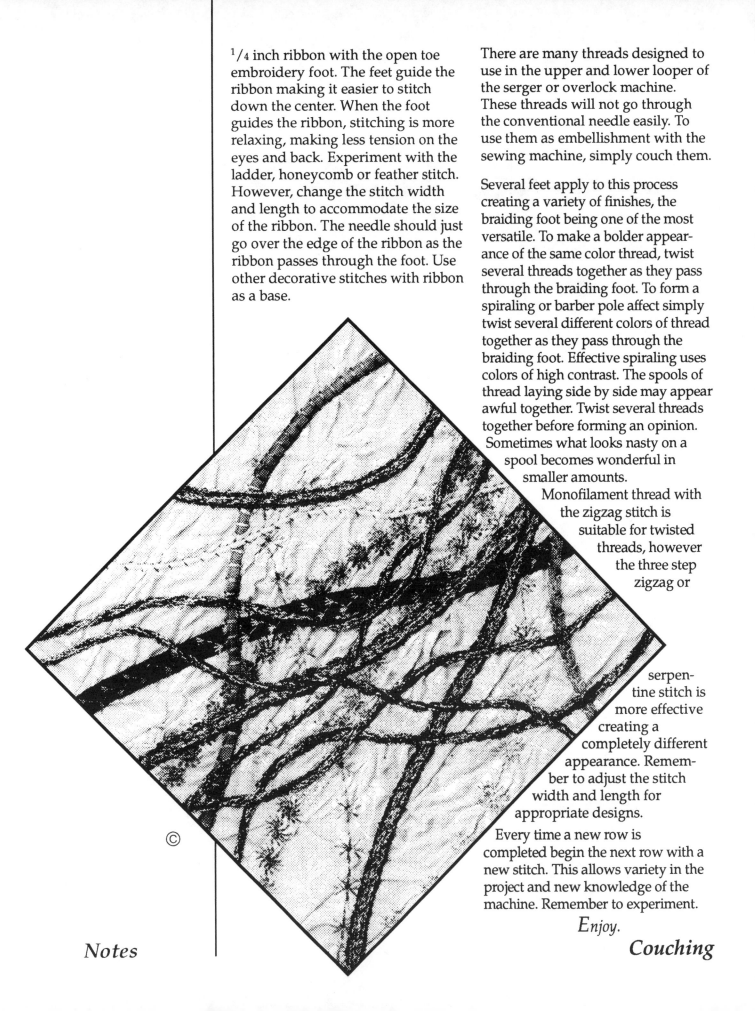

^{1}/4 inch ribbon with the open toe embroidery foot. The feet guide the ribbon making it easier to stitch down the center. When the foot guides the ribbon, stitching is more relaxing, making less tension on the eyes and back. Experiment with the ladder, honeycomb or feather stitch. However, change the stitch width and length to accommodate the size of the ribbon. The needle should just go over the edge of the ribbon as the ribbon passes through the foot. Use other decorative stitches with ribbon as a base.

There are many threads designed to use in the upper and lower looper of the serger or overlock machine. These threads will not go through the conventional needle easily. To use them as embellishment with the sewing machine, simply couch them.

Several feet apply to this process creating a variety of finishes, the braiding foot being one of the most versatile. To make a bolder appearance of the same color thread, twist several threads together as they pass through the braiding foot. To form a spiraling or barber pole affect simply twist several different colors of thread together as they pass through the braiding foot. Effective spiraling uses colors of high contrast. The spools of thread laying side by side may appear awful together. Twist several threads together before forming an opinion. Sometimes what looks nasty on a spool becomes wonderful in smaller amounts. Monofilament thread with the zigzag stitch is suitable for twisted threads, however the three step zigzag or serpentine stitch is more effective creating a completely different appearance. Remember to adjust the stitch width and length for appropriate designs.

Every time a new row is completed begin the next row with a new stitch. This allows variety in the project and new knowledge of the machine. Remember to experiment.

Enjoy.

Notes

Couching

*A*nother consideration for heavier threads while couching are the cording feet. Various feet are designed for different machines. But all machines have cording feet with three to seven holes or grooves. The different cording feet are used primarily to embroider several heavier threads at once, resulting in a multicolored design much like a ribbon illusion. The different holes align the threads perfectly. Practical or decorative stitches produce special effects.

Couching Too

Ordinarily all holes in the foot are threaded at once. But just because there are a number of holes in a foot does not mean that all holes must be used at the same time. Creativity happens when rules are broken. Sometimes only the outer holes are used with a decorative stitch set to the widest. Other times odd holes are used allowing space between the lines of heavier thread. Incorporate a variety of uses from the same foot into the same project. Every row stitched can be a different application.

Always apply the widest, flattest embellishments first. As the layers progress add the more bulky layers like edgestitched ribbon, beads and sequin yardage.

Narrow ribbon ¹/₄ inch and wider has more opportunities than ever. The edgestitching foot permits accurate sewing along one edge. When the ribbon is couched in wavy lines, the curves add extra dimension. Use a straight or decorative stitch just over one edge of the ribbon making the other edge

move into outer space. Two rows of ribbon may be attached at one time, much like combining the laces with heirloom sewing. Both sides of the ribbon may be attached or one side left to float.

Sequins should be applied before beads since they are the flatter of

the two. It is easy to meander sequins over a

project intersecting when the design requires. With a monofilament thread in the needle and the open toe foot, zigzag over the sequins. Set the stitch width slightly wider than the sequin size, preventing the needle from piercing the sequin. The stitch length should be identical to the width. Because there is a nap to sequin yardage, the smooth direction should be placed so that it runs with the foot. After applying the sequins, glide your finger over the sequins, making the monofilament thread move between the sequin overlap. Presto, there is no monofilament thread showing.

A corded piping, or Pearls 'N Piping foot allows Cross-Locked or molded bead yardage to pass through the machine avoiding a mishap. They are sewn quickly with little effort using the proper technique. Machine settings will vary depending on bead size. Place a row of beads in the groove of the foot and hand-walk the machine through the stitch to be certain the needle clears the bead. The settings are a little bit wider and a little bit longer than the bead so that the needle does not touch the bead in the stitching process. The monofilament thread will slide off the bead, making the stitching virtually impossible to see.

The easiest way to prevent mishaps with beads is to never sew any closer to a previous row of beads than the width of the presser foot. It is possible to cross beads, but do it very carefully.

Oh, sew easy!

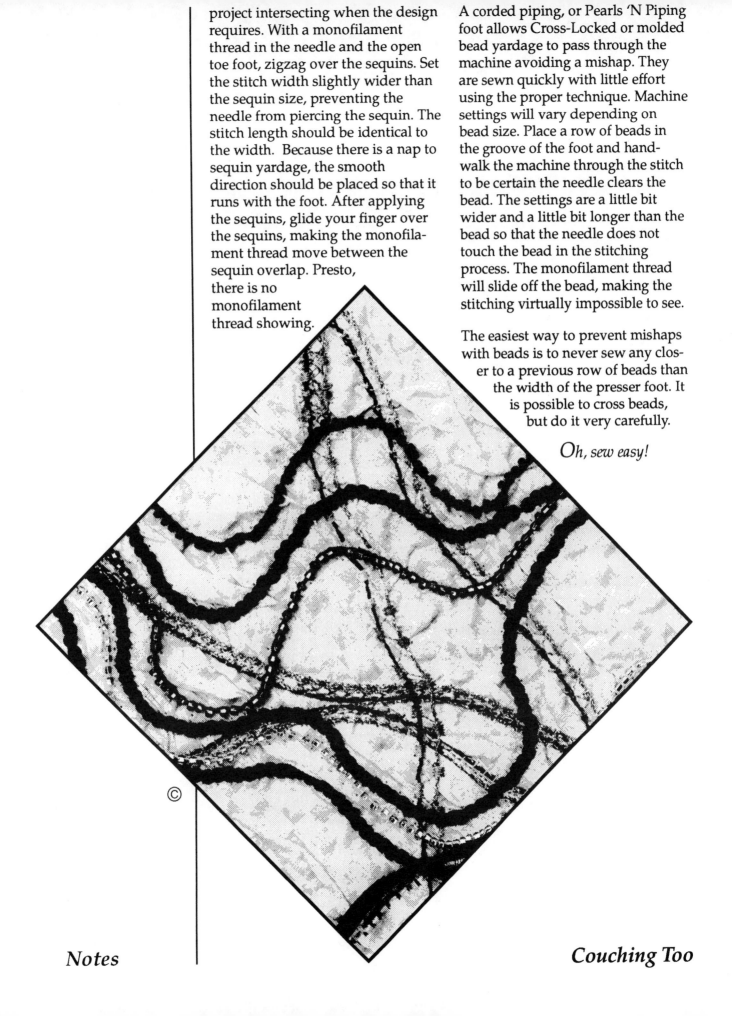

Notes

Couching Too

Fringe It

There are so many stitches on the new sewing machines from which to choose . But the fun begins when the playing starts. With a few new approaches or a little incentive, even utility stitches become embellishment. It is so much fun to change the rule and make something different than it was originally intended.

Take a look at the grass or irregular satin zigzag stitch. Using two decorative threads in a topstitching needle fills in the stitch to make it fuller. The open toe embroidery foot allows the layers of stitching to pass under the foot easier. Some of the variegated threads, particularly those that do not match in color variety are considerably different when sewn through the same needle. Or choose a variegated thread in combination with a solid color thread. Change the stitch width and length slightly rather than conform to the machine settings. Meander over the fabric whether flat or crinkled giving the fabric a slight tug from side to side while the machine is in motion. A delicate pull will not strain the needle or machine in any way.

After completing the first row of stitching, add another row close or almost parallel to the first. Sometimes overlap the stitches and other times allow the fabric to peek through forming a braid appearance. Several rows may be stitched in this manner for wider braid. Consider making several

©

rows of braiding illusion each having varying widths.

Using the same two spools of thread and the same stitch, switch to a 2.0 double needle. Test or hand walk the machine through the stitch to be sure the double needle clears the presser foot. Add a few more rows of stitching creating a different appearance. The double needle keeps the threads separated to differentiate the separate colors, while the single needle overlaps the thread in a single stitch.

Switch to the fringe or tailor tacking foot. Set the machine for narrow to medium zigzag to clear the bar on the foot. Place both threads in the topstitching needle and loosen the tension to almost zero. As the needle stitches over the bar in the foot extra loops or fringe is formed. Tie off the threads

before beginning by stitching in position. Fill in the blank areas of fabric with this dimensional stitch. Some of the rows may be stitched the full length of the project while others may be small areas. When a row of stitching is complete, tie off the threads and lift the presser foot and pull the last few stitches from the bar area of the foot. The options are endless.

Enjoy the fun of creating new texture.

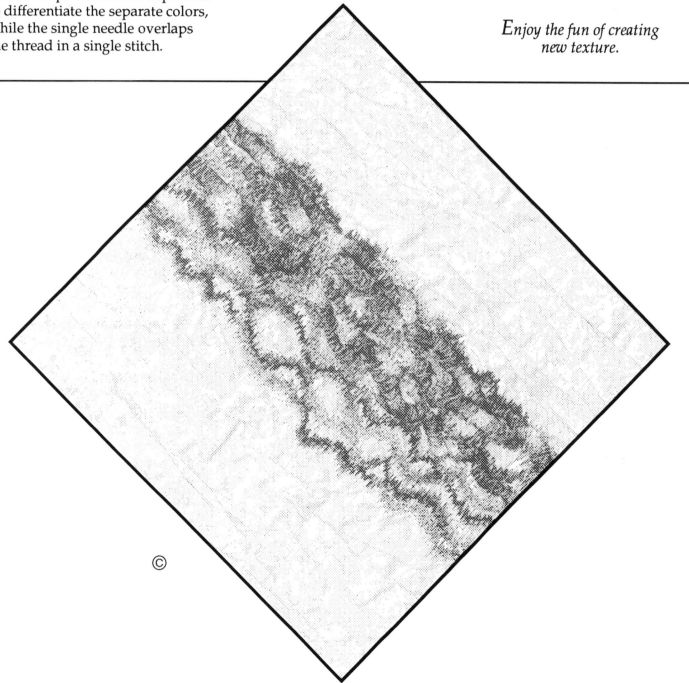

*I*t is relatively simple to make pintucks using a double needle and a pintuck foot. To speed the process when making rows of pintucks, form the length of fabric into a tube overlapping the crosswise grain edges about one inch. Stitch to hold in place.

Cotton embroidery thread in the needles and bobbin make beautiful pintucks as well as some of the decorative threads in the needle. Start the stitching process on the overlapped seam with a 2.0 double needle and a 7 groove pintuck foot. Stitch completely around using the edge of the tube as a guide to maintain a straight line in the first row. When the beginning of the first stitching is reached allow the first row of stitching to align with another groove on the foot. Continue in this manner making all changes in the grooves at the overlapped seam. A symmetrical system can be established or an irregular design.

Experiment with a few decorative stitches and the double needle. Be very careful to test the stitch width to avoid breaking needles. There are buttons on most machines for this purpose. The feather stitch is excellent in the double needle. Continue the pintucking procedure throughout the fabric tube. When the pintucking is complete, cut along the original straight stitched, overlapped line to create a large piece of pintucking.

Paper backed miniature quilt blocks are easy and accurate to incorporate into designs. Flying geese, one of the quickest traditional patterns uses only triangle shapes. Fabric is placed on the blank side of the paper pattern. Stitching is done on the printed side of the pattern using a tiny stitch length.

The first fabric is placed on the blank side of the pattern right side up, covering the piece marked #1. Any foot that provides the most visibility of the printing is the appropriate one for this procedure—straight stitch or $^1/_4$ inch. Using a

Pintuck *With a* Goose

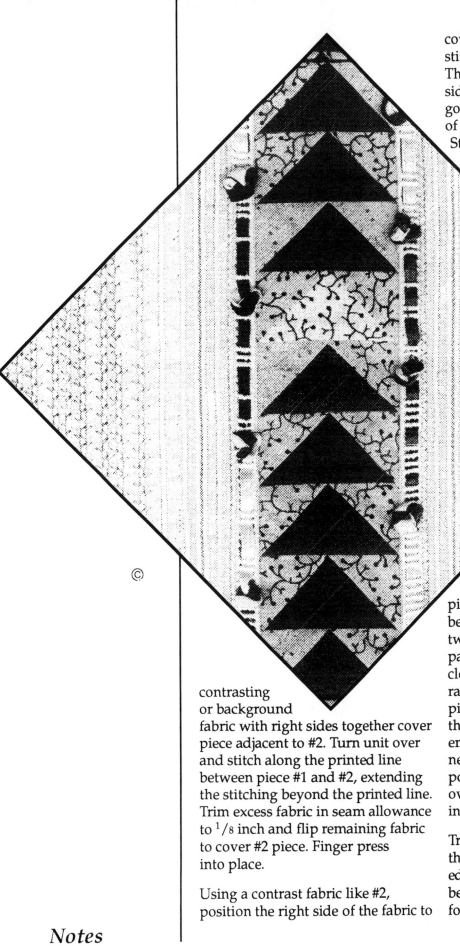

cover piece beside #3. Follow the stitch, trim, flip and press procedure. The second #1 piece is placed right sides together covering the previous goose pattern, allowing a minimal of fabric in the seam allowance. Stitch along the longer stitch line between the two patterns. Again follow the trim, flip and press procedure to continue the flying geese pattern. Do not pull paper away from fabric until the design has

been inserted into a finished position of final project.

There are two options to combine the elements of pintucking with flying geese using beading to join. The less bulky of the two is used when the beading is parallel to the pintucks. Trim very close to the last pintuck. If the fabric ravels, roll and whip over the last pintuck with a small zigzag using the edgestitch foot and cotton embroidery thread. It may be necessary to change the needle position such that the needle goes over the pintuck with the zig and into outer space for the zag.

Trim the extra batiste from one side of the beading. Continuing with the edgestitch foot, butt the edge of the beading to one side of the bar on the foot and the rolled pintuck to the

contrasting or background fabric with right sides together cover piece adjacent to #2. Turn unit over and stitch along the printed line between piece #1 and #2, extending the stitching beyond the printed line. Trim excess fabric in seam allowance to $1/8$ inch and flip remaining fabric to cover #2 piece. Finger press into place.

Using a contrast fabric like #2, position the right side of the fabric to

other side of the bar. Zigzag over the two pieces adjusting the width and length when necessary so that the zig goes into the hole of the beading and the zag goes over the pintuck. Minor changes in stitch width and length keep the holes clean and open.

The other side of the beading is attached in a different manner. It is used to combine sections of embellishment that are bulky and cannot be rolled. This is another use for the edgestitching foot. With the beading on top, right sides together, match the outer point of the flying geese with the outer ridge of the beading. Align the bar of the edgestitching foot to the right ridge of the beading. This will act as a guide, making the stitching position accurate. Move the needle position to the right and stitch approximately $1/16$ of an inch from the ridge.

With either of these techniques the bar of the edgestitching foot acts as a guide for accuracy, the beading is exposed to the maximum and little bulk

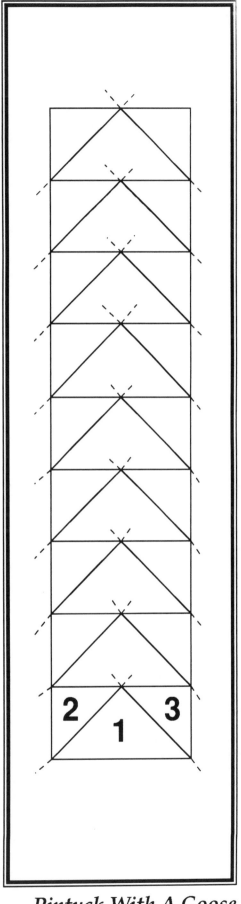

remains in the seam allowance.

Weave a single or double layer of ribbon through the holes in the beading to emphasize extra color. The weaving may be irregular with occasional knots for added design. Small tricks like this add designer touches, creating one of a kind.

It is so much fun.

Notes

Pintuck With A Goose

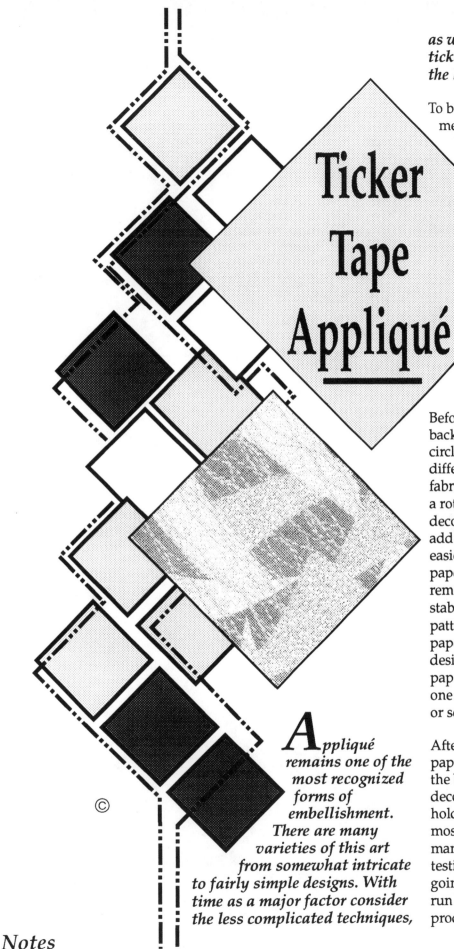

Ticker Tape Appliqué

as well as the most fun. This puts ticker tape appliqué at the top of the list.

To begin, press paper backed fusing medium like Transfer Fusing™ or Wonder Under™ to the wrong side of appliqué fabric using the wool setting on a dry iron. Keep in mind that the wrong side of a fabric could easily become the right side if you so choose. It is proper to have both sides of the fabric showing in the same project. Sometimes this is just the right contrast for variety.

Before removing the paper from the back, cut irregular shapes such as circles, triangles, stars, etc. in different sizes from the appliqué fabric. Use scissors, pinking shears, a rotary cutter, or some of the decorative wavy rotary blades to add character to the design. It is easier to cut the shapes with the paper on rather than the paper removed because there is more stability. Another option is to draw pattern designs directly on the paper. One word of caution—the design should be drawn on the paper with a mirror image when a one way design is desired like letters or sewing machine designs.

After cutting the shapes, remove the paper from the appliqué. Position on the background fabric in a decorative manner and steam to hold in place. Steam works best with most fusibles on the wool setting of many irons. Avoid a problem by testing with scrap fabric before going to the real project. Many irons run hotter than others. They also produce different amounts of steam.

*A*ppliqué remains one of the most recognized forms of embellishment. There are many varieties of this art from somewhat intricate to fairly simple designs. With time as a major factor consider the less complicated techniques,

©

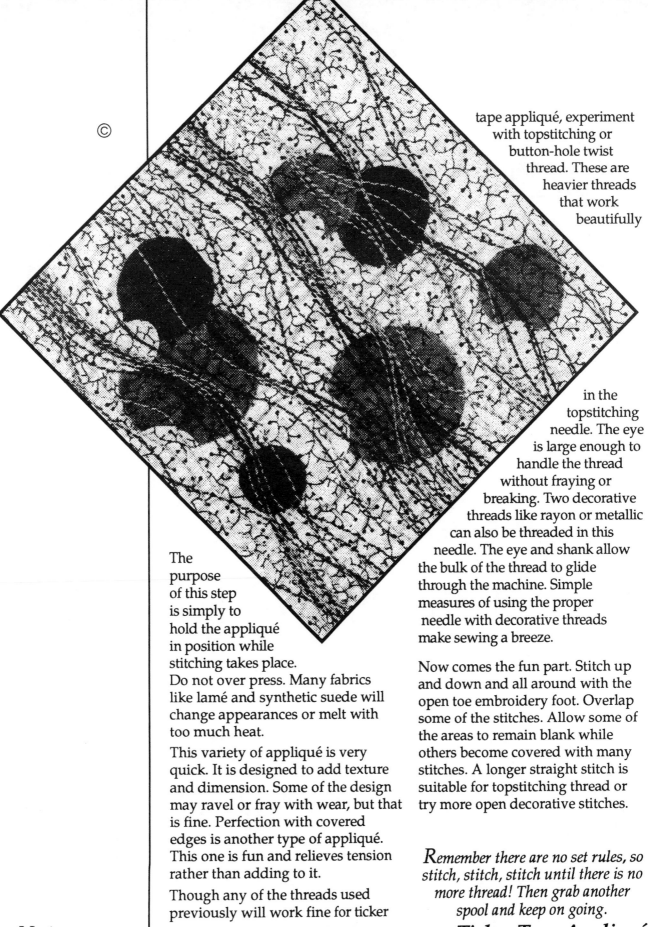

tape appliqué, experiment with topstitching or button-hole twist thread. These are heavier threads that work beautifully in the topstitching needle. The eye is large enough to handle the thread without fraying or breaking. Two decorative threads like rayon or metallic can also be threaded in this needle. The eye and shank allow the bulk of the thread to glide through the machine. Simple measures of using the proper needle with decorative threads make sewing a breeze.

Now comes the fun part. Stitch up and down and all around with the open toe embroidery foot. Overlap some of the stitches. Allow some of the areas to remain blank while others become covered with many stitches. A longer straight stitch is suitable for topstitching thread or try more open decorative stitches.

Remember there are no set rules, so stitch, stitch, stitch until there is no more thread! Then grab another spool and keep on going.

Ticker Tape Appliqué

The purpose of this step is simply to hold the appliqué in position while stitching takes place. Do not over press. Many fabrics like lamé and synthetic suede will change appearances or melt with too much heat.

This variety of appliqué is very quick. It is designed to add texture and dimension. Some of the design may ravel or fray with wear, but that is fine. Perfection with covered edges is another type of appliqué. This one is fun and relieves tension rather than adding to it.

Though any of the threads used previously will work fine for ticker

Notes

A spill of soft pintucking charms any outfit with uncommonly rich texture of shadows and double needle stitching. They can be refined and delicate on a very sheer fabric. Or more rounded and dimensional with a heavier fabric. But, pintucking with updated methods is truly one of the easiest forms of texture.

Pintucking in the round (the Pintuck with a Goose chapter) makes pintucking much simpler with uncomplicated rows of perfectly parallel pintucks. But many times that method makes too many or takes too long to cover a certain portion of a project. So why not meander all over the fabric using the same feet and needles? It covers more territory, makes wonderful intersections, forms little framed areas for other embellishments, and uses less time.

Just as updating other types of needle work requires a few extra tips and tricks, so does pintucking. Because there is no way of judging how much fabric the tucking will use, begin with a piece at least one third larger than the expected finish size. The fabric should be relatively soft to form the tucks. If it is very sheer or soft, spray starch and press the fabric first for body. The starch prevents the light weight fabric from gathering in the grooves of the foot and forming larger or uneven tucks.

The pintucks could be corded or not. They could use embroidery rayon or cotton, silk, metallic, lamé or other thread. The needle size and width distance can vary according to the type of fabric and thread or desired finished appearance. A good starting point is a 2.0 size 80 needle with the 7 groove pintuck foot.

It is always easier to begin and end on the edge of the fabric. There are no untidy ends to contend with! Be certain the presser

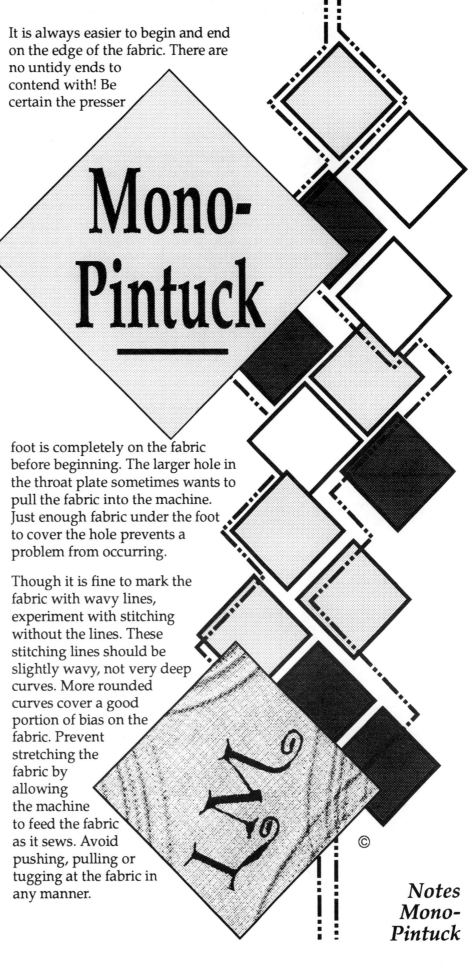

Mono-Pintuck

foot is completely on the fabric before beginning. The larger hole in the throat plate sometimes wants to pull the fabric into the machine. Just enough fabric under the foot to cover the hole prevents a problem from occurring.

Though it is fine to mark the fabric with wavy lines, experiment with stitching without the lines. These stitching lines should be slightly wavy, not very deep curves. More rounded curves cover a good portion of bias on the fabric. Prevent stretching the fabric by allowing the machine to feed the fabric as it sews. Avoid pushing, pulling or tugging at the fabric in any manner.

Notes
Mono-
Pintuck

Meander over the fabric to an edge. Stop with the needle in the up position. Lift the presser foot and pull the fabric about an inch to prevent the next row from gathering at the beginning. Then lower the presser foot aligning the previous row of stitching in one of the grooves. Continue stitching perfectly parallel rows of wavy pintucks. Sew several rows which are parallel but not necessarily evenly spaced, then form another wavy line which intersects the previous one. The overlapping areas are always different shapes and sizes depending upon the angles they intersect. These are unexpected designer touches which can add to the artistic arrangement of the composition.

The spaces formed where there is no stitching are perfect little framed areas for monograms, decorative stitch combinations, or enlarged programmed stitch designs. Not every area needs to be filled with a design, but a few of the larger areas warrant a cluster of added stitches. It is the perfect place to show off features of the machine.

Experiment. Think of the fun you are going to have!

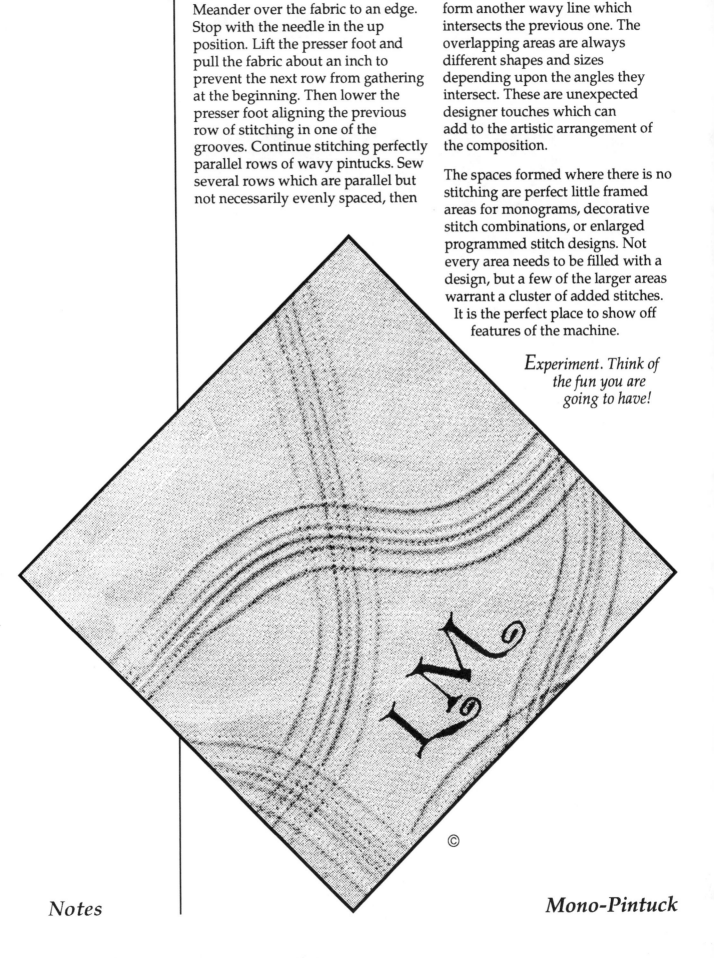

Notes

Mono-Pintuck

Traditional Appliqué
Made Easy

Stitch these shapes in the same manner as the leaf appliqué (Lesson 11). Allow the outer edge to float while the stitching is in the center. Take for instance the long squiggle and spiral shapes. Because the shapes are so narrow and long, the tendency is for the piece to shift while stitching, even though the piece is fused in place. To prevent shifting, stitch a straight line down the center to hold in position and return over the same line with a satin stitch. Determine the stitch width by the proportion of the pattern width. This stitching is quick, easy and half as much stitching.

Consider the asterisk shape. The three rows of satin stitches intersect in the center. This design is complete in seconds, whereas mitering the eighteen corners would take minutes longer.

The five point star and heart are stitched using the width of the presser foot as a guide. Double check the opening of the foot.

*A*s the adventure with appliqué continues, geometric designs like the patterns enclosed could again become very time consuming when the shape is stitched on the outer edge. Notice the number of corners and points in each design. Why resort to the more complicated, traditional stitching procedure when it is actually more fun and less time consuming to use another artistic approach.

Sometimes the needle position should be changed to the right on wider open feet to make the stitch closer to the cut edge. Other times the foot is narrow and it is not necessary to make a change. Experiment and enjoy the freedom to change when a different design is desired for the proportion of the appliqué.

Notes

Traditional Appliqué

©

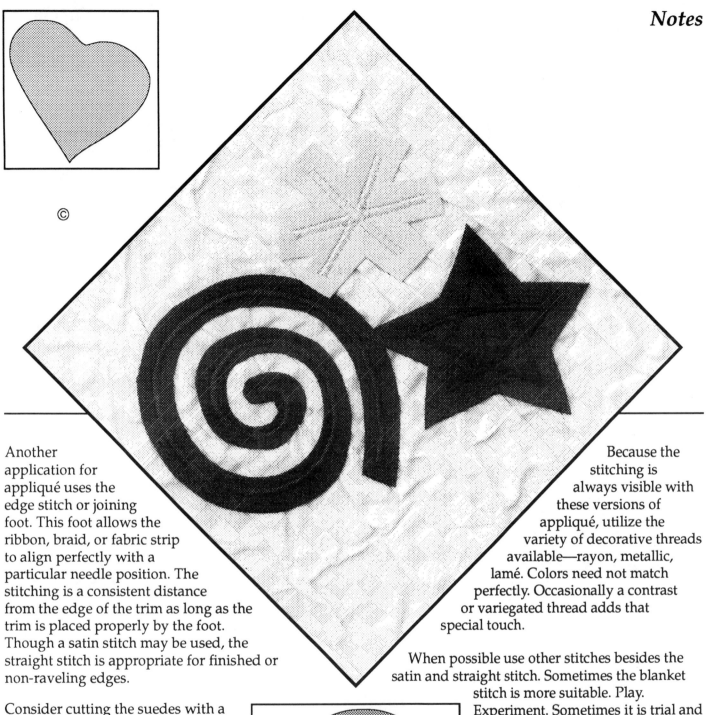

Another application for appliqué uses the edge stitch or joining foot. This foot allows the ribbon, braid, or fabric strip to align perfectly with a particular needle position. The stitching is a consistent distance from the edge of the trim as long as the trim is placed properly by the foot. Though a satin stitch may be used, the straight stitch is appropriate for finished or non-raveling edges.

Consider cutting the suedes with a wavy or pinking shape. Whether the scissors or rotary version is used, each has its own distinctive appearance. Or, work with woven fabrics which may take a more textured look. Cut holes in the strips using the key hole punch from the button hole set. Leather tools offer a larger variety of hole sizes, each adding to the scheme of the pattern.

Because the stitching is always visible with these versions of appliqué, utilize the variety of decorative threads available—rayon, metallic, lamé. Colors need not match perfectly. Occasionally a contrast or variegated thread adds that special touch.

When possible use other stitches besides the satin and straight stitch. Sometimes the blanket stitch is more suitable. Play. Experiment. Sometimes it is trial and error. But this is all part of creativity and learning new techniques.

The needle is always an important factor when stitching. The embroidery needle is best with decorative threads like rayon, metallic, and lamé. Choose a needle size which corresponds to the type of fabric—a smaller size needle

Traditional Appliqué

for lightweight fabrics and larger needle for heavier fabrics.

Another alternative refers to the amount of thread going through the needle. Sometimes a heavier appearing thread would make the appliqué more artistic or dimensional. Two rayon, metallic, or lamé threads will glide through the top stitching needle with ease. A slightly longer stitch length may be used, however the stitching fills in better with two threads as opposed to one. This achieves a different effect than working with a top stitching thread because the two threads are softer.

No matter which fabric and thread are applied, appliqué is a wondrous adventure leading to hours of enjoyment at the sewing machine. It is okay to experiment with several appliqué ideas and stitching procedures on the same project.

Continue to explore.

Cutwork: Form of embroidery where portions of the foundation fabric are cut away from the background of the design. Lace like effects can be obtained by increasing the number of cut spaces. Buttonhole stitch by hand or satin stitch by machine are an integral element for this art work.

Traditional Cutwork has long been an exquisite, time consuming embroidery process. Careful stitching, cutting and additional stitching form this sometimes dainty, artistic hand or machine needlework. Just as other needle arts are made easier with new products and procedures, the same is true with cutwork, making it as simple to create as other sewing methods.

One of the most crucial steps with cutwork is carefully trimming the fabric around the design without cutting into the stitches. A fabric remover known as FIBER-ETCH™ can expedite the process. FIBER-ETCH™ is a sewing/craft aid to cleanly remove plant fibers: Cotton, Linen, Ramie, Rayon and Paper for cutwork and reverse appliqué as well as within open areas of iron on appliqué, embroidery, or painted areas of fabric.

Apply a thin layer of FIBER-ETCH™ to the area to be removed, dry with a hair dryer, iron press with a wool setting to remove plant fibers, and rinse under running water to eliminate any residue. The FIBER-ETCHed area drops out of the fabric leaving a hole. The FIBER-ETCH™ is far more accurate and precise than trimming and cutting tiny bits and pieces of fabric.

Caution: Because FIBER-ETCH™ removes plant fibers only, the stitching threads for the project should not be plant matter. Use Silk, Metallic without rayon core, Nylon, Polyester, or Acrylic threads.

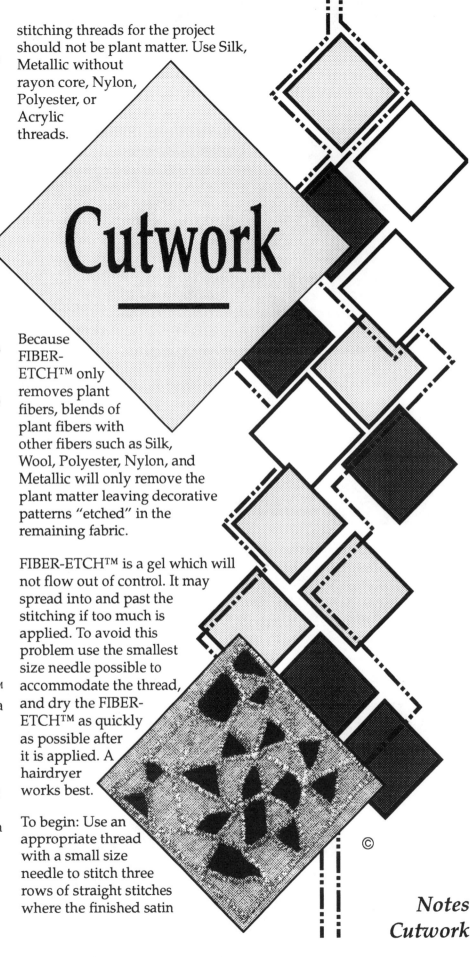

Cutwork

Because FIBER-ETCH™ only removes plant fibers, blends of plant fibers with other fibers such as Silk, Wool, Polyester, Nylon, and Metallic will only remove the plant matter leaving decorative patterns "etched" in the remaining fabric.

FIBER-ETCH™ is a gel which will not flow out of control. It may spread into and past the stitching if too much is applied. To avoid this problem use the smallest size needle possible to accommodate the thread, and dry the FIBER-ETCH™ as quickly as possible after it is applied. A hairdryer works best.

To begin: Use an appropriate thread with a small size needle to stitch three rows of straight stitches where the finished satin

©

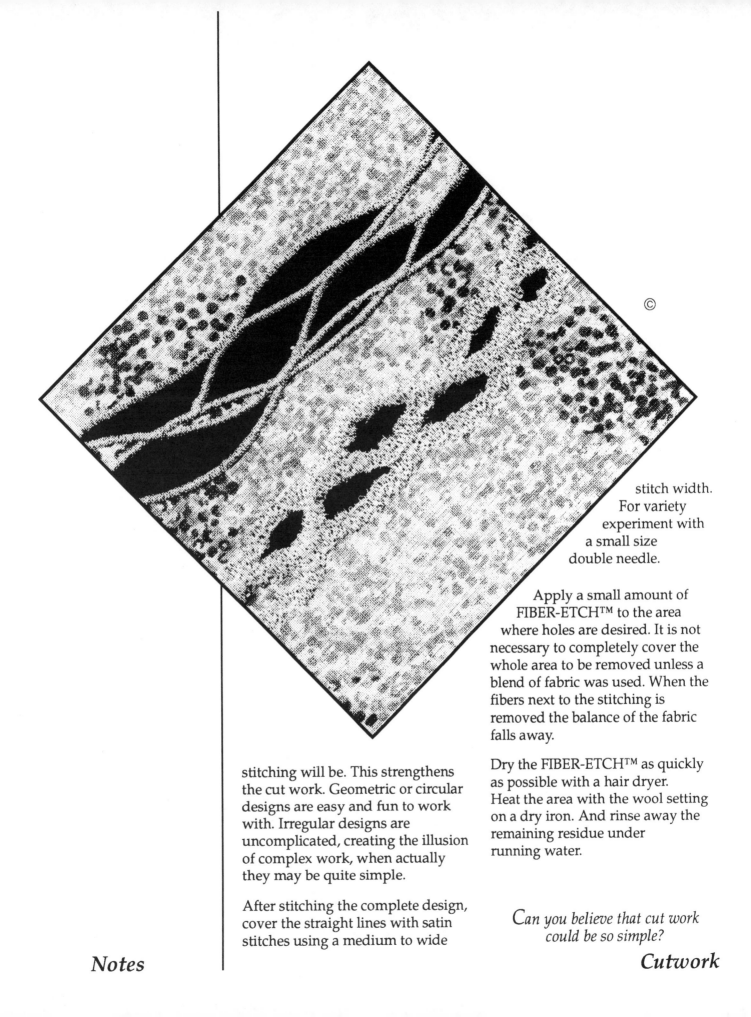

stitch width.
For variety
experiment with
a small size
double needle.

Apply a small amount of
FIBER-ETCH™ to the area
where holes are desired. It is not
necessary to completely cover the
whole area to be removed unless a
blend of fabric was used. When the
fibers next to the stitching is
removed the balance of the fabric
falls away.

Dry the FIBER-ETCH™ as quickly
as possible with a hair dryer.
Heat the area with the wool setting
on a dry iron. And rinse away the
remaining residue under
running water.

stitching will be. This strengthens
the cut work. Geometric or circular
designs are easy and fun to work
with. Irregular designs are
uncomplicated, creating the illusion
of complex work, when actually
they may be quite simple.

After stitching the complete design,
cover the straight lines with satin
stitches using a medium to wide

*Can you believe that cut work
could be so simple?*

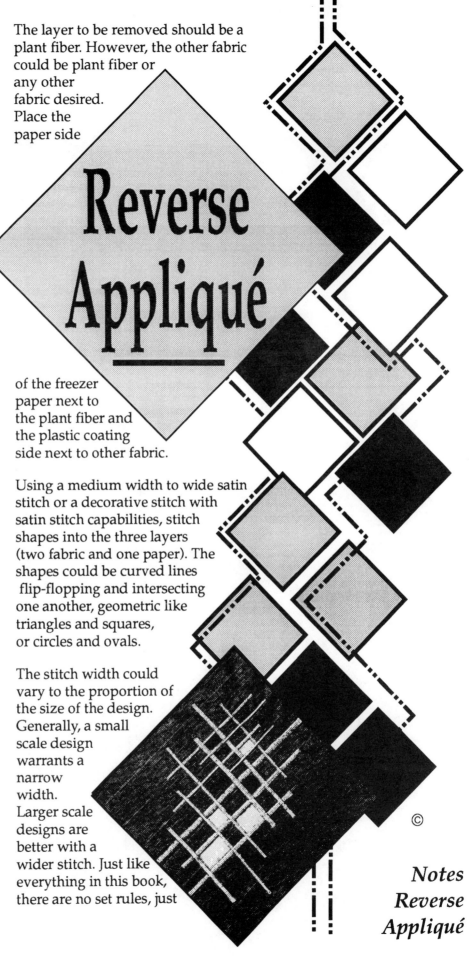

Before beginning this section, review the chapter on Cutwork. FIBER-ETCH™ is used to produce this new version of appliqué. The new fabric removal product is explained in detail in this chapter. For your benefit it is important that you understand the procedure with FIBER-ETCH™ before starting any reverse appliqué.

R*everse Appliqué: A process where several layers of different colors and/or types of fabric are stitched together with satin stitches to form one fabric. The layers are then trimmed to expose the under layers giving a variety of colors to the piece.*

Reverse Appliqué is another form of embroidery where modern conveniences make the process less complicated and easier to produce. To make reverse appliqué many hours of tedious cutting and trimming take place. By using FIBER-ETCH™, the process is far less difficult.

FIBER-ETCH™ removes plant fibers. This includes paper. However, special paper is necessary to prevent the FIBER-ETCH™ from removing all layers of fabric. Freezer paper has a plastic coating which does not disappear with application of FIBER-ETCH™. Freezer paper is desired rather than a layer of plastic since the paper layer absorbs any extra FIBER-ETCH™ which may have penetrated through the fabric. The pressing process with FIBER-ETCH™ removes the top layer of fabric and paper, leaving the plastic to simply peel off exposing the remaining fabric.

To begin this project, layer freezer paper between two layers of fabric.

The layer to be removed should be a plant fiber. However, the other fabric could be plant fiber or any other fabric desired. Place the paper side of the freezer paper next to the plant fiber and the plastic coating side next to other fabric.

Using a medium width to wide satin stitch or a decorative stitch with satin stitch capabilities, stitch shapes into the three layers (two fabric and one paper). The shapes could be curved lines flip-flopping and intersecting one another, geometric like triangles and squares, or circles and ovals.

The stitch width could vary to the proportion of the size of the design. Generally, a small scale design warrants a narrow width. Larger scale designs are better with a wider stitch. Just like everything in this book, there are no set rules, just

©

Notes Reverse Appliqué

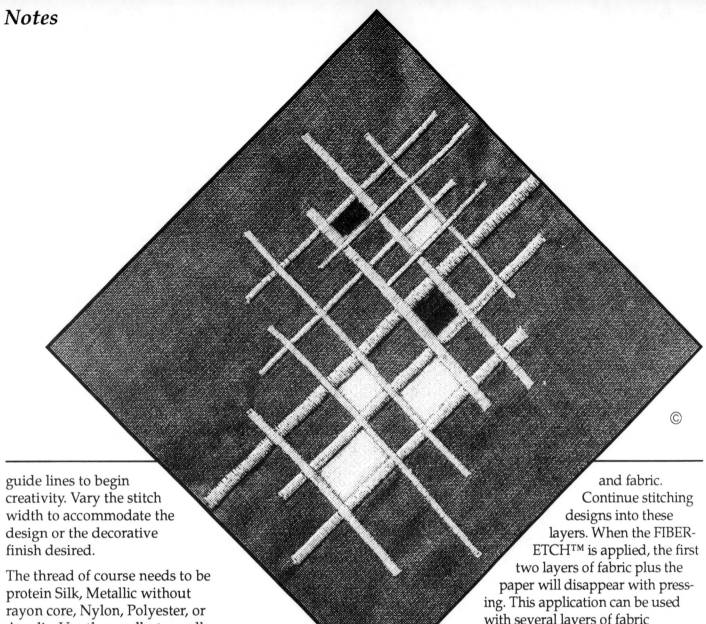

guide lines to begin creativity. Vary the stitch width to accommodate the design or the decorative finish desired.

The thread of course needs to be protein Silk, Metallic without rayon core, Nylon, Polyester, or Acrylic. Use the smallest needle size possible to accommodate the thread. Larger sized needles make larger holes in the fabric allowing the FIBER-ETCH™ to spread more than necessary.

Once the stitching process is complete, apply FIBER-ETCH™ to the area where the fabric should be removed. Dry the FIBER-ETCH™ as quickly as possible to prevent the gel from spreading too far. A hair dryer works best. Use the wool setting on a dry iron to press the fabric until the FIBER-ETCHed area falls out. Peel the plastic layer from the fabric to produce a dimensional, varied colored piece.

This method allows two fabrics in the project. However, sometimes several layers of color and fabric may be desired. To do that, each layer must be plant fiber with exception of the final layer.

Stitch two layers of fabric and freezer paper together at a time following the procedure for reverse appliqué. Once the design is stitched, pressed, and the fabric and freezer paper are removed, add an additional layer of freezer paper

and fabric. Continue stitching designs into these layers. When the FIBER-ETCH™ is applied, the first two layers of fabric plus the paper will disappear with pressing. This application can be used with several layers of fabric depending upon the weight of the fabric.

For extra security or special effects, apply additional stitching to the design. Satin stitching worked close to another row of satin stitching creates a ribbon affect. Once the FIBER-ETCHing is complete, variegated rayon thread can add more illusion.

A fresh mix of texture and color make for an ingenious answer to easy stitching.

Reverse appliqué has never been so easy.

Reverse Appliqué

Leaf Appliqué

T *he most common method of appliqué uses satin stitches (zig zag stitch with short stitch length) around the outer edge of the fabric being applied to the base. Though this method can be fairly easy to accomplish, some patterns have many curves, corners and points. These are the areas which require expertise or perfection, and sometimes use more time than desired for a small project.*

It can be just as attractive, add more dimension, and less time consuming to stitch within the pattern rather than the border of the appliqué.

Take for instance this simple leaf pattern. The inside and outside curves are relatively sharp making the stitching very tedious particularly with a wide satin stitch. Rather than stitch around the outside edge of the design, stitch only the veins with a satin stitch allowing the outer edges to hang loose. Use a stitch width that is proportional to the size of the leaf itself, usually, $1^1/2$ to 2. This width is easier to turn and manipulate.

Consider the starting point. Typically, the stem appears to be the most logical beginning. However, study the veins. Naturally, the tiny veins branch from a larger vein to nothing at the tip of the leaf. This could easily become the design in the appliqué making each leaf appear alive. With stitching solely in the veins and stem, the outer edges of the leaf are loose, free and floating just as they are falling from a tree.

Adapt this idea to the sewing machine. By turning the stitch width knob from wide to narrow or nothing, the stitching could look similar to a natural leaf. But there are so many points extending from the same vein. Follow the sequence on the pattern. Begin with a satin stitch width of $1^1/2$ to 2 and sew to nothing at the point. The tiny straight stitches at the point finish the end. The beginning is covered by the next row of stitches.

The progression of this process may appear a little odd at first but after making several leaves, the finished product is smoother, quicker, and

Notes

more natural. The wider beginning stitches are concealed by the curves in future veins. It is less complicated to sew from wide to narrow than it is from narrow to wide. Remember to keep it simple.

Synthetic suedes like Ultra Suede® and Lamous make wonderful appliqués. They do not ravel. But there is no reason why a woven fabric cannot be used with this same technique. Use several layers of fabric for one leaf or transfer this same idea into a flower. The layers add dimension and the ravels add texture.

Consider the variety of threads for the needle. Fine cotton embroidery thread adds sheen. Rayon adds a nice shine.

©

Leaf Appliqué

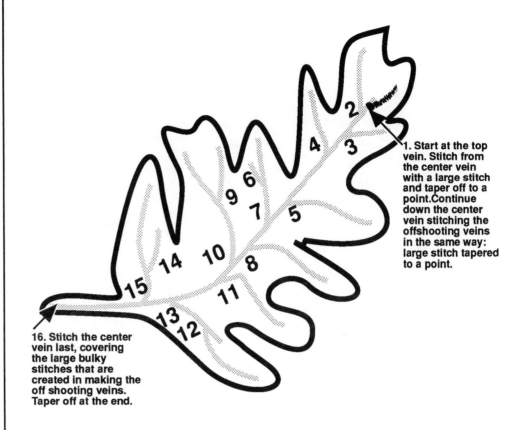

1. Start at the top vein. Stitch from the center vein with a large stitch and taper off to a point.Continue down the center vein stitching the offshooting veins in the same way: large stitch tapered to a point.

16. Stitch the center vein last, covering the large bulky stitches that are created in making the off shooting veins. Taper off at the end.

Metallic and lamé add glitz. Determine the desired finished appearance and use the needle thread accordingly. Typically the best needle is the embroidery needle to avoid thread breaking problems.

Because so much thread is used in appliqué, fill the bobbin with bobbin thread or cotton embroidery thread. It is a finer thread, allowing the bobbin to hold more, with less frequency in changing the bobbin. If an extra filled bobbin is handy, the empty one can be replaced quickly without cutting the needle thread. Stitching continues with a nice even flow. There is no starting and stopping to fill bobbins, just

changing to a full bobbin when one is empty.

The process of appliqué requires a special sewing foot. The front area of the open toe appliqué foot permits the stitcher to view every corner, curve, and point as they appear, improving precision stitching. The bottom of the foot contains a small flat groove permitting the stitching to flow to the back of the foot without build up or bulk. The proper foot makes the application easier.

Take pleasure in creating a new version of appliqué!

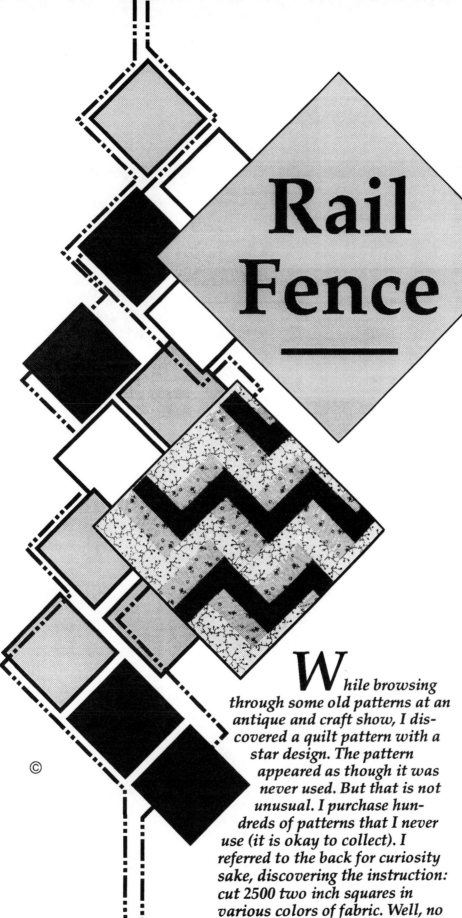

Rail Fence

used. It would take ages to cut so many two inch squares, count them, and sew them back together again!

Piecing of quilts has taken major transformation from our Grandmother's quilts. Rather than cut so many tiny pieces, fabric strips are used. Several strips may be stitched together before the piece is recut, reassembled and stitched again. The process is quite simple and not nearly as involved as expected.

One of the traditional quilt patterns, the rail fence, goes together quickly with the stripping method. The basic cutting and stitching does require a certain amount of accuracy. Use the rotary cutter and a see-thru ruler to cut three or four 1-inch strips of fabric (45 inches wide). Because the finished piece will be so small for this project it is recommended that the fabric have small to little design. The fabric collection should contain color range from light, medium, and dark. Arrange the strips in a pleasing manner.

Sew the strips together with a $1/4$-inch seam allowance using the edge of the presser foot as a guide. There are $1/4$-inch presser feet available for all machines on the market as well as generic feet that fit most machines. Some feet have advantages over others or slight architectural differences. The most important factor to remember is to use a consistent seam allowance throughout the project. Any time the cutting and seam allowances shift, the finished piece is irregular. Try to maintain consistency.

Press the seam allowances toward the darker fabric. The strip should be flat with no extra pleats and tucks.

*W*hile browsing *through some old patterns at an antique and craft show, I discovered a quilt pattern with a star design. The pattern appeared as though it was never used. But that is not unusual. I purchase hundreds of patterns that I never use (it is okay to collect). I referred to the back for curiosity sake, discovering the instruction: cut 2500 two inch squares in various colors of fabric. Well, no wonder the pattern was never*

©

Measure the width of the strip from cut edge to cut edge. This is the size the blocks will be cut. Cut the strip into square blocks maintaining accuracy. If the ruler slips while cutting, true the square and continue cutting. There is plenty of fabric for this size project. Better to trash a square than work with a crooked square!

Place the squares on the table in the manner shown with one square vertical and the next one horizontal. One strip should form a zigzag through the piece. Sew the blocks together in sections rather than long strips to maintain accuracy.

The stripping method is very quick when constructing many quilt patterns. Each pattern has a basic rule. Then play with the design factor. For a larger project use wider strips remembering to allow $1/4$-inch seam allowances on each side of the strip. With wider strips the fabric design could vary from small to larger designs.

Though three or four strips were mentioned at the beginning of the chapter, six or eight strips with colors running from light to dark make a nice rail fence. Of course this many strips will go into a larger project.

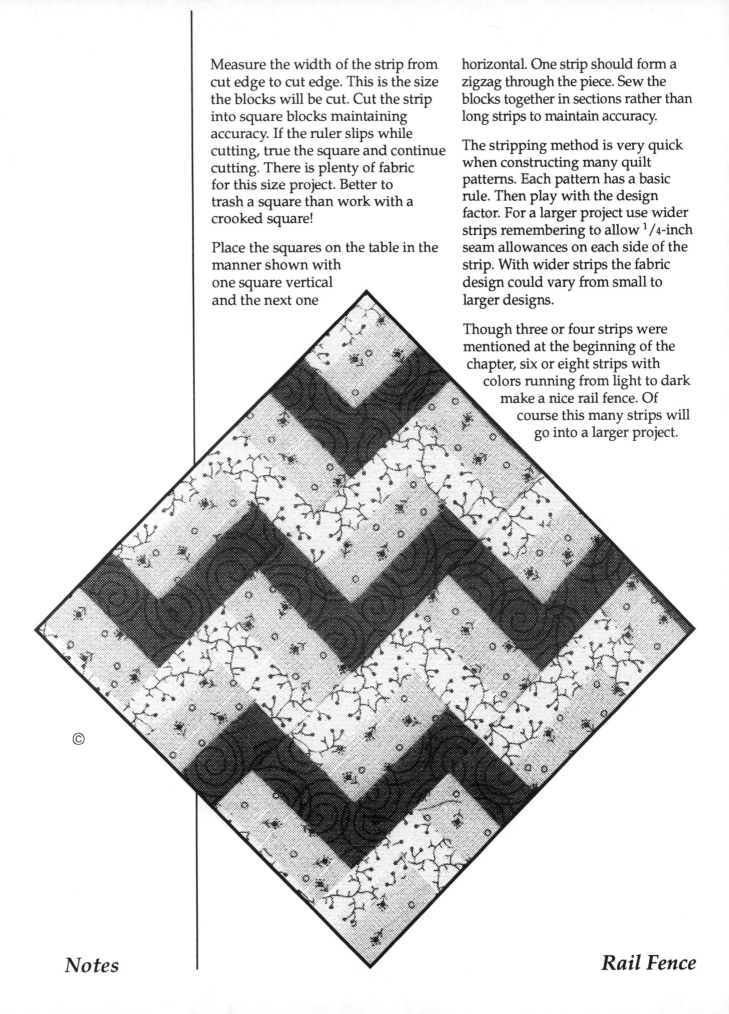

Notes

Rail Fence

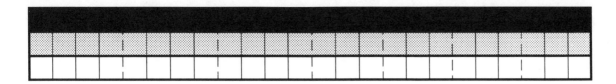

Two sets of strips could be very effective for a rail fence. Use two dark fabrics, two medium fabrics, and one light fabric for the piece. Each strip would contain the same light fabric along with a medium and dark.

The road to quick stripping is easy. The finished piece is quickly assembled. Use the rail fence as an inset on accessories, in a garment, as a wall hanging, baby quilt, or full size quilt. It is one of the quickest traditional patterns.

Piecing is an adventure. No matter what the fabric looks like on the bolt, it always changes its appearance cut up.

It's fun!

(To the left) Color the blocks with coloring pencils to explore different variations possible for the rail fence.

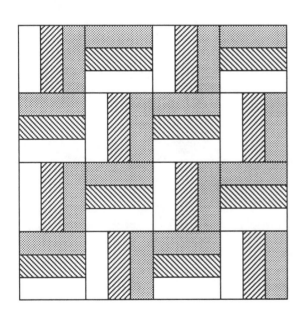

(To the right) Two sets of strips with dark and medium fabrics, each grouping having the same light.

©

Notes
Rail Fence

*T*he easiest way to avoid problems of sizing when texturing or making special effects with fabric is to always make more than necessary. It is simple to cut down a piece to the size required, yet very disappointing to come up short. No matter which is the case, whether trimming down, adding more to size up, or using leftovers to build another project, use something to separate the sections, to give each segment its own framework, yet not dominate the entire piece.

Corded piping segregates the different segments or designs, yet gives each area definition and dimension. Each portion has its own border, before another technique begins. For variety and color use double or triple corded piping. Remember that the boundary around each element should accent or outline the work rather than overpower the composition.

Other ways to edge a segment are braid, ribbon, strips of fabric and other trims. With lightweight fabrics, sew the sections together with a conventional seam allowance. Stitch the trim to cover the seam line. Simple!

Heavier fabrics are treated differently. Butt the two edges together so that raw edges meet. There should be little to no space between to cause a weak or thin area. Cover the raveling area with a trim. The zigzag stitch forms a stronger finish than the straight stitch in most cases.

Use the wavy or pinker blade with the rotary cutter set to cut Ultrasuede® or other types of fabric. Place a bonding medium (Wonder Under or Transfer Fusing) on the base fabric before cutting the narrow strips. Cut the strips in different widths for

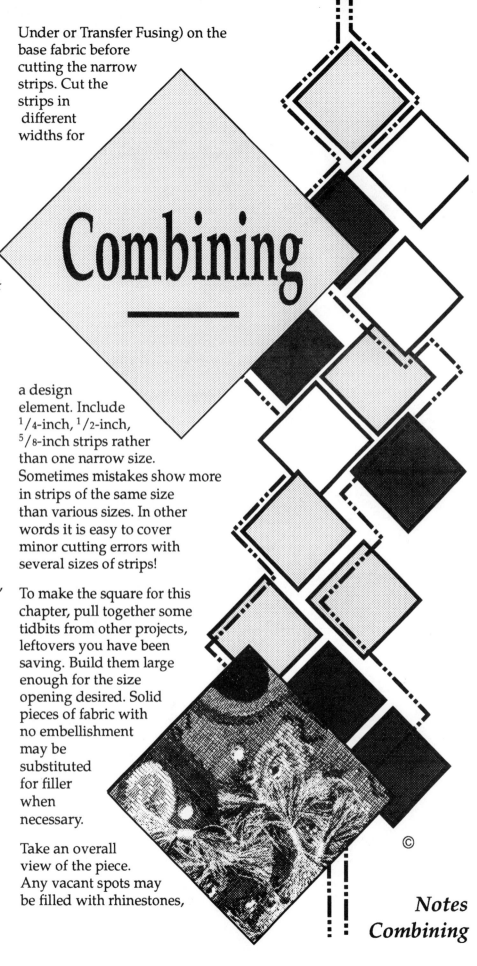

Combining

a design element. Include $1/4$-inch, $1/2$-inch, $5/8$-inch strips rather than one narrow size. Sometimes mistakes show more in strips of the same size than various sizes. In other words it is easy to cover minor cutting errors with several sizes of strips!

To make the square for this chapter, pull together some tidbits from other projects, leftovers you have been saving. Build them large enough for the size opening desired. Solid pieces of fabric with no embellishment may be substituted for filler when necessary.

Take an overall view of the piece. Any vacant spots may be filled with rhinestones,

©

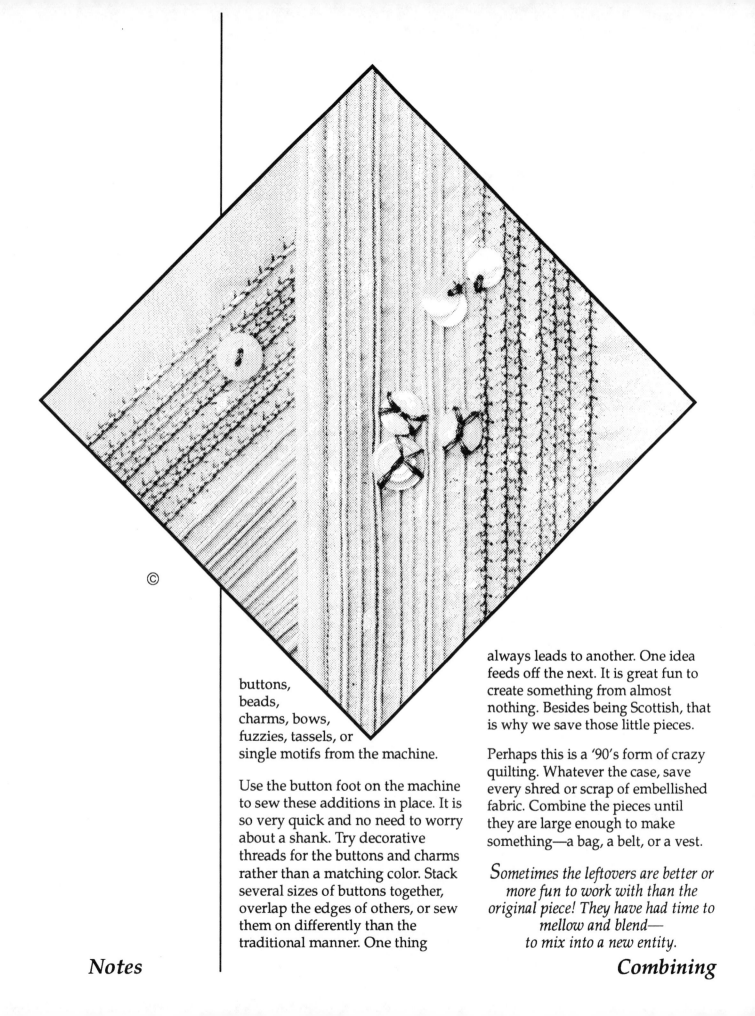

©

buttons,
beads,
charms, bows,
fuzzies, tassels, or
single motifs from the machine.

Use the button foot on the machine to sew these additions in place. It is so very quick and no need to worry about a shank. Try decorative threads for the buttons and charms rather than a matching color. Stack several sizes of buttons together, overlap the edges of others, or sew them on differently than the traditional manner. One thing always leads to another. One idea feeds off the next. It is great fun to create something from almost nothing. Besides being Scottish, that is why we save those little pieces.

Perhaps this is a '90's form of crazy quilting. Whatever the case, save every shred or scrap of embellished fabric. Combine the pieces until they are large enough to make something—a bag, a belt, or a vest.

*Sometimes the leftovers are better or more fun to work with than the original piece! They have had time to mellow and blend—
to mix into a new entity.*

Putting
it all
together

**Handbag Instructions,
Cutting Layout
and Pattern**

*Putting It
All Together*

Cameo Shuffle

The mock cording inset or cameo shuffle makes the possibilities for embellishment endless. The fake pocket permits other insets to be exchanged within the same base. These basic instructions are incorporated into the Portfolio Handbag Pattern. They could very easily with adaptations be transformed into a variety of handbag patterns, accessories, or garments. An oval is given in this pattern though a circle, square, or odd shape would alter the appearance for many different looks.

Yardage and Notions

8 Inch	Straight Hex-Open Frame	1 Pair Circular Posts (to hold strap)
$1/2$ Yard	(45" Wide) Fashion Fabric	1 Pair Snapper Rings (to hold chain)
$3/8$ Yard	Fleece	Thread
$3/8$ Yard	Fusible Web	
$3/8$ Yard	Lining	*The bag is appropriate in crisp fabrics such as*
$3/4$ Yard	Fusible Interfacing	*tapestry, brocade, ticking, denim, or synthetic suede.*

Pattern Instructions

Step 1: To make the cameo shuffle, mark the oval on wrong side of mock cording fabric (#4). Position right side of cording fabric on right side of fashion fabric (#1) matching notch at top. Use a short stitch length ($1^1/2$—2) to stitch the oval overlapping the beginning and ending with several stitches to secure and avoid bulk.

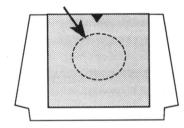

Step 2: Trim to $1/16$ inch for tightly woven fabrics but no wider than $1/8$ inch.

Step 3: Turn cording fabric through hole to allow just an edge (no more than

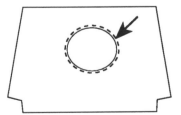

$1/8$ inch) of cording fabric to show. The narrow trimmed seam allowance fills the cording area making the ridge look as though there is corded piping. Stitch in the ditch with the edgestitching foot to hold cording in place.

Step 4: On wrong side of corded hole, center embellished square over opening.

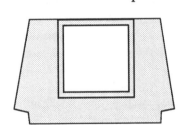

The square should be $1/4$ inch smaller than cording fabric. Trim as necessary.

Step 5: Place fusible web (#1) between wrong side of fashion fabric with cameo, and fleece (#1). Fuse together by using wool setting on steam iron and wet press cloth. This step will form a permanent pocket for other embellishments. The mock cording has the illusion of corded piping though there is none.

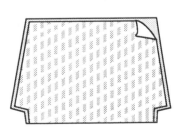

Handbag Instructions

Step 6: Place right sides together at fold line. Stitch side seams.

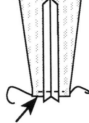

Pattern Instructions

Step 7: Miter corner by matching side seam to bottom fold. Stitch.

Step 8: Fuse interfacing casing (#3) to wrong side of fashion fabric casing (#3). Fold ends of casing wrong sides together at $1/2$ inch as pattern shows and fuse using scraps of fusible web. Fuse facing interfacing (#2) to wrong side of fashion fabric facing (#2).

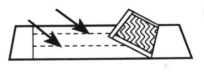

Step 9: Position casing on facing matching small dots with wrong side of casing to right side of facing. Stitch along upper and lower edges at $3/4$ inch leaving ends open.

Step 10: Fuse lining interfacing (#5) to wrong side of lining (#5). Stitch casing-facing to lining matching notches. Press seam allowances towards lining section.

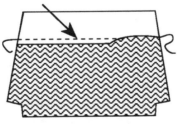

Step 11: Place right sides of lining and facing together. Stitch side seams leaving opening for turning. Stitch miter as in Step 7.

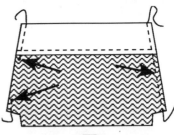

Step 11: Continued from left column (Diagram to the left)

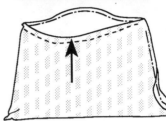

Step 12: With right sides together (one inside the other), stitch upper edge of handbag to upper edge of facing.

Step 13: Turn right side out through opening. Slipstitch opening.

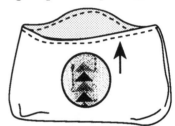

Step 14: Topstitch upper edge at $1/4''$ to hold facing inside handbag.

Step 15: Slide straight hex-open frame through casing. Press ends of frame together to align holes. Slide self-piloting rivets through ends of frame. Sometimes it is easier to use pliers to hold the frame while installing the rivets.

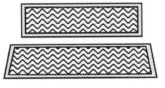

OPTIONS

To attach a chain directly to the frame, use snapper rings instead of self-piloting rivets.

When a strap is preferred, use circular posts to secure strap to handbag.

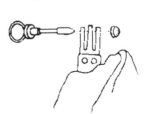

Welcome the chance to make a professional looking handbag.

Handbag Instructions

Cutting Layout Fashion Fabric

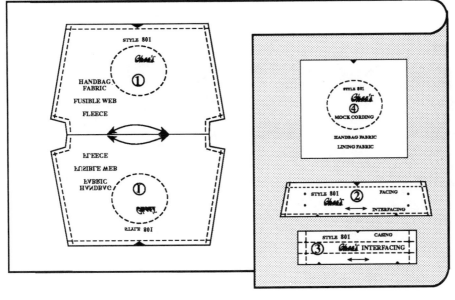

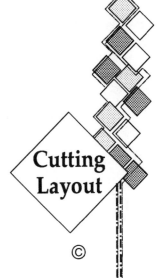

Fleece and Fusible Web or Fusible Fleece

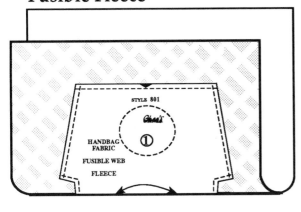

Fusible Interfacing

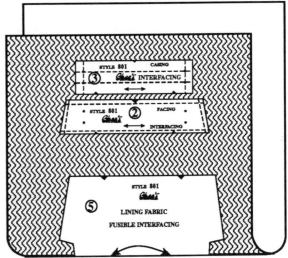

Lining

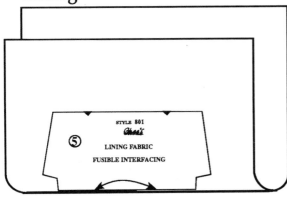

Check with your local stores for the availability of Ghee's products. If they are not available, please contact Ghee's for ordering information.

Ghee's offers a variety of handbag patterns along with the metal frames, magnetic snaps, chains, dog clips, lock sets and other hardware to make them. The Prestige Collection #401 uses the doctor frame available in 3 sizes. The Cameo Clutch #601 uses an angle vanity frame, available in 7 sizes. The Hobo Tote #751 and Empress #771 use a curved hex-open frame, available in 3 sizes. The portfolio #801 and cosmetic, clutch & tote #851 use the straight hex-open frame available in 12 sizes. The Saunter Satchel #901, Classic Eloquence #951 and Picturesque Heirloom #971 use the tubular frame available in 5 sizes.

Linda McGehee's books, "Texture With Textiles" and "More...Texture With Textiles" with creative, detailed, embellishment and techniques, are also available. Use Linda's vest #693 as a base to show off any of these ideas.

ISBN# 09637160-1-8

A Companion Project Book for Texture With Textiles 1994 is a trademark of Linda F. McGehee. All rights reserved. Printed in the United States of America. No part of this book may be used or reproduced in any manner whatsoever without written permission except in the case of brief quotations embodied in critical articles and reviews.

Ghee's®

2620 Centenary Blvd. #3-205
Shreveport, LA 71104
(318) 226-1701